Flying Machines

Use the stickers at the end of this section to complete each page.

hinkler

Passenger aircraft

These aircraft are huge and can carry many people long distances. Have you ever flown in an aircraft?

Passenger aircraft reach amazing heights!

An airport has many runways.

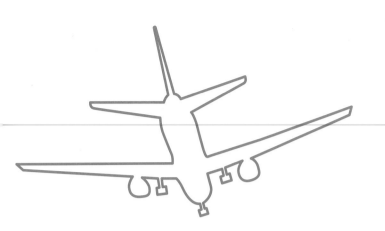

The pilot flies the aircraft using these controls.

Hot-air balloons

Hot air keeps these balloons in the air.
How many can you see?

Helicopters

Helicopters have long blades that spin very fast. Can you count how many blades are on each helicopter?

Blackbird

This is the fastest aircraft in the world.
It can travel to the edge of space!

The blackbird is used by NASA
for aeronautical research.

The blackbird requires a
parachute to slow down.

Let's fly

Look at all the different aircraft.

How many helicopters can you see?

Space shuttle

3, 2, 1, BLAST OFF! When in space, the space shuttle orbits the earth.

the moon

The space shuttle can deliver
satellites into space.

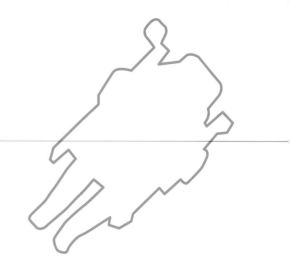

This astronaut is going
for a space walk.

The space shuttle needs a
parachute to slow down.

This jumbo jet can carry
the space shuttle.

Transport aircraft

This transport aircraft can carry very heavy cargo.

This aircraft opens in half, to help get its cargo in and out.

Solar-powered aircraft

This long aircraft gets its power
from the sun.

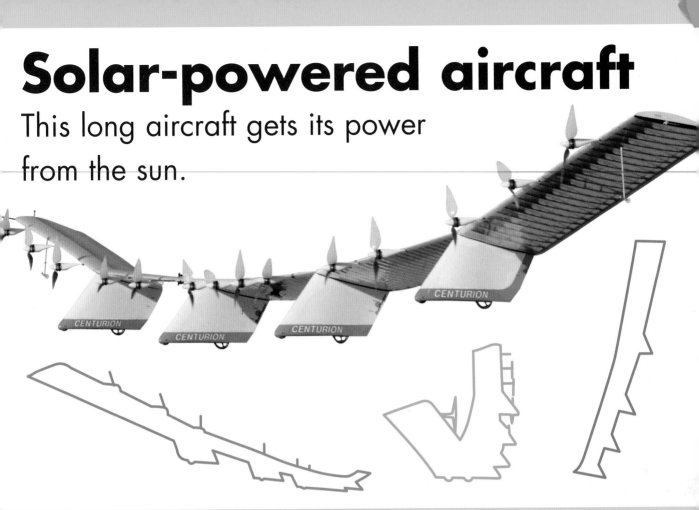

Single propeller

This small aircraft's propeller rotates, producing force.

Aircraft parts

Look carefully at the boxes. Can you match which part goes with which aircraft?

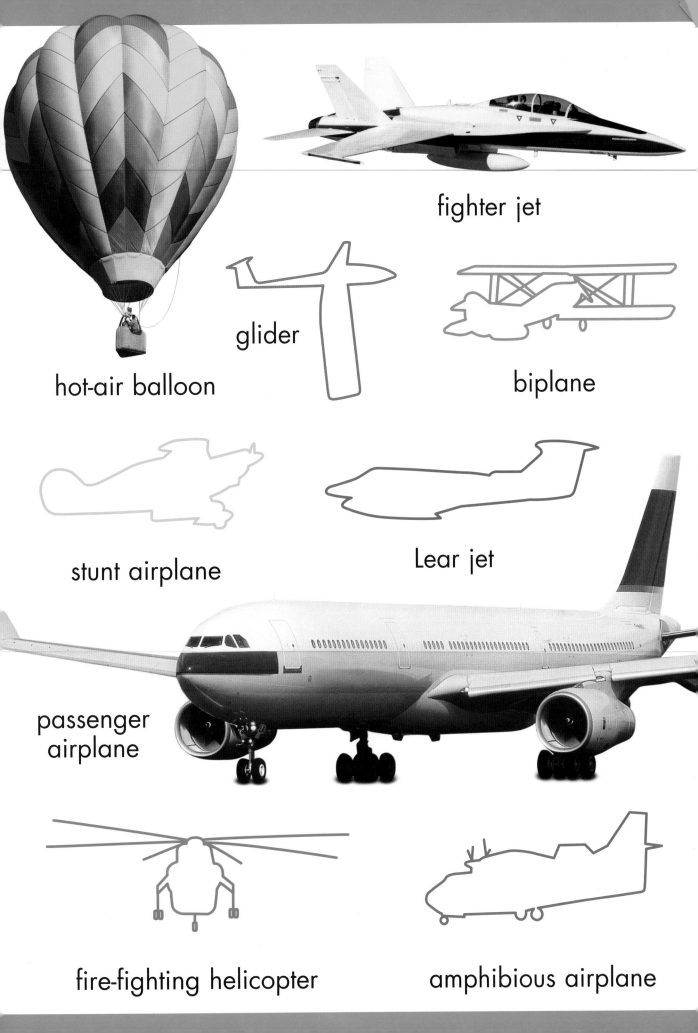

fighter jet

glider

biplane

hot-air balloon

stunt airplane

Lear jet

passenger airplane

fire-fighting helicopter

amphibious airplane

Wild Animals

Use the stickers at the end of this section to complete each page.

Elephant

Elephants are the largest animals on land.
They use their trunk to grab food.

Elephants
love to play
in water.

Lion

A group of lions is called a pride. A male lion's bushy hair is called a mane.

These lionesses are looking after their cubs.

Wolf

A wolf is a wild dog that loves to hunt. A group of wolves is called a pack.

Giraffe

The giraffe is the tallest animal on Earth.
Its long neck helps it reach the treetops.

Tiger

The tiger is the largest member of the cat family. Tigers live in forests and woodland and are excellent swimmers.

Bald eagle

The bald eagle has very sharp claws called talons. It uses them to grab its prey.

The bald eagle loves to catch fish.

Hippopotamus

The hippopotamus spends most of its time in water. Its large teeth are called tusks.

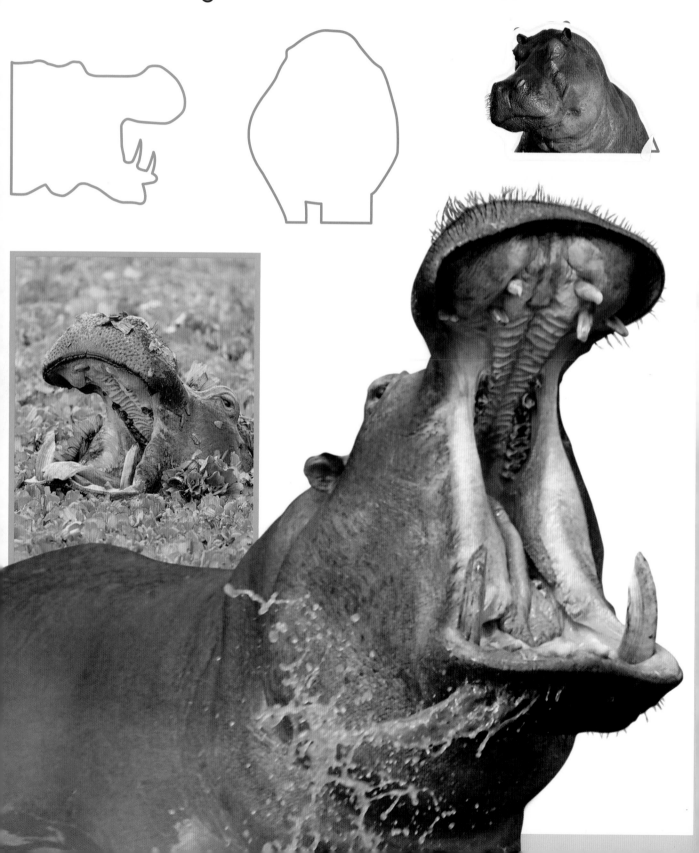

Cheetah

The cheetah is the fastest runner on Earth.
Wild cheetahs can only be found in Africa.

Polar bear

The polar bear lives in the icy Arctic. Its white fur camouflages the bear in the snow.

Zebra

The zebra is a wild horse with black and white stripes. It lives in a large group called a herd.

Rhinoceros

The rhinoceros is an endangered species. It has poor eyesight and one or two horns on its snout.

Mighty Movers

Use the stickers at the end of this section to complete each page.

Giant wheel loader

Look at the size of this machine's scoop!
It can lift huge amounts of rock.

The giant scoop moves up and down.

Garbage truck

This truck helps to keep our homes clean. It picks up dumpsters full of garbage and takes them away.

The garbage is picked up and dumped in the back of the truck.

Cement mixer

This truck mixes cement and delivers it to a construction site.

The cement is mixed in the big barrel.

Track excavator

This excavator's undercarriage has a tracked wheel.
The big extendable arm is used for digging.

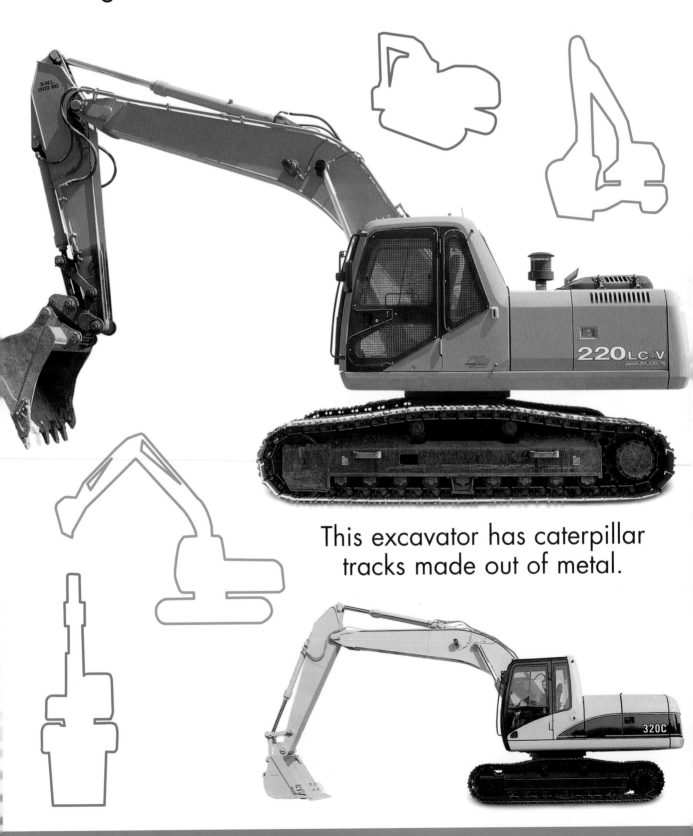

S.W.L.
1500 KG

220 LC-V

This excavator has caterpillar
tracks made out of metal.

320C

Tractor

Tractors are most often used on farms.

This tractor has a digger that moves up and down.

Dump truck

Dump trucks are used to transport materials.
Can you find the stickers that go on this page?

The giant loader
fills the dump truck
up with dirt.

Mobile crane

A mobile crane is used to lift workers high in the air. What could you reach if you had one of these?

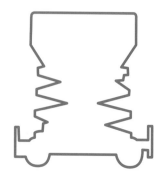

Grader

This machine has a long blade that is used to scrape dirt flat when building roads.

Transporters

These huge trucks transport goods long distances.

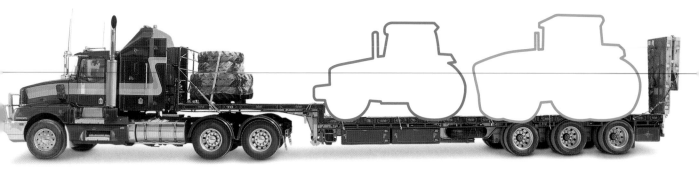

Semitrailer

A semitrailer is a dump truck with two trailers.

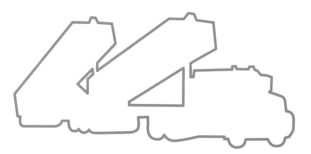

Rig

Rigs are big trucks that pull heavy loads.

This rig can tilt forward to reveal the engine.

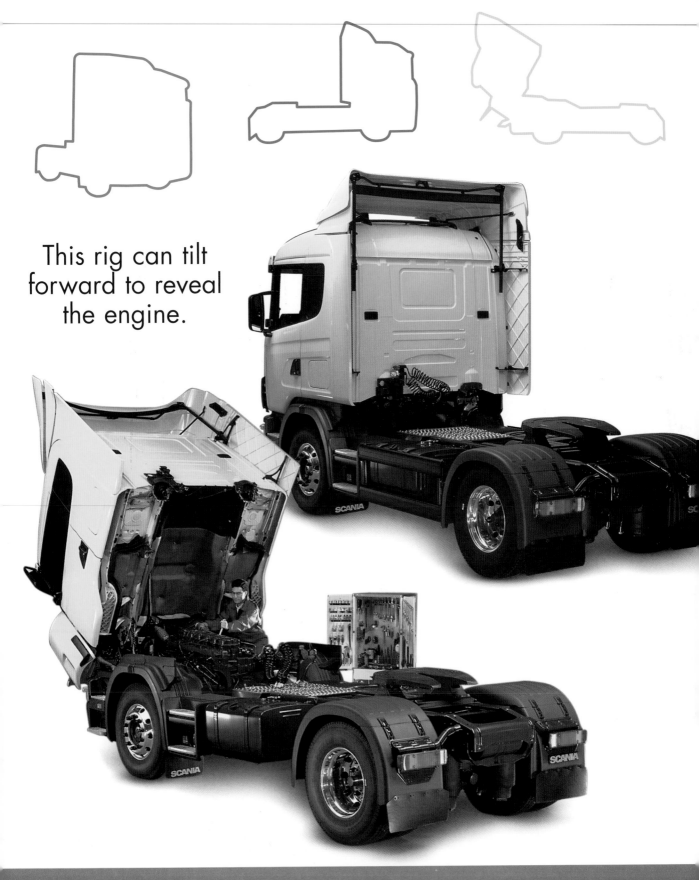

Mighty machines

Look at all of the mighty machines in action! Can you find the missing half to complete the picture?

tractor

treaded tractor

mobile
crane

giant dump truck

Insects
and Bugs

Use the stickers at the end of this section to complete each page.

Butterflies and moths

Look at all the bright colors on these frisky flyers! Can you find the missing stickers?

Beetles

Beetles are the most common insects. They can be found living all over the world.

Grasshoppers

These insects have strong hind legs and can jump a long way.

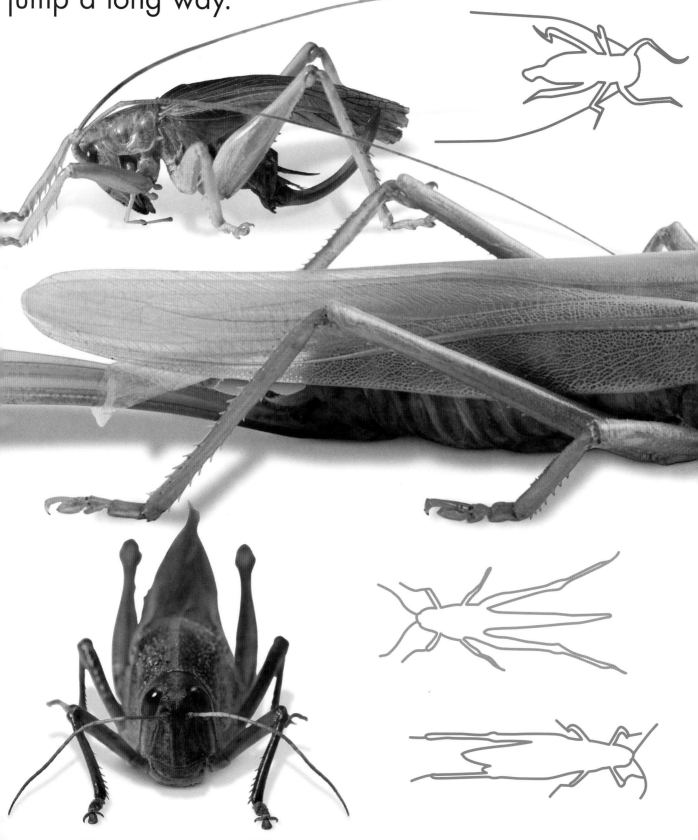

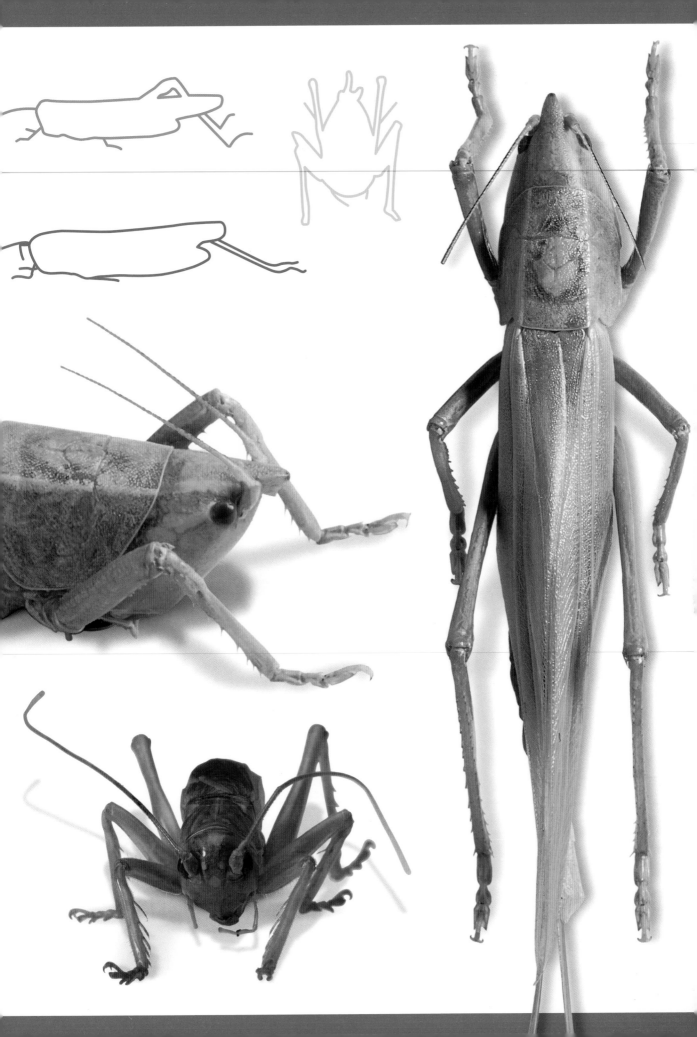

In the garden

Insects and bugs love flowers. Can you find the missing stickers?

Praying mantis

This insect is harmless to us but other insects beware! The praying mantis has very sharp spikes on its front legs to capture food!

Dragonflies

These flyers have large eyes and four wings.
They can fly forward and backward!

More insects and bugs

Look at all the different insects and bugs. Which insect looks like a twig on a tree?

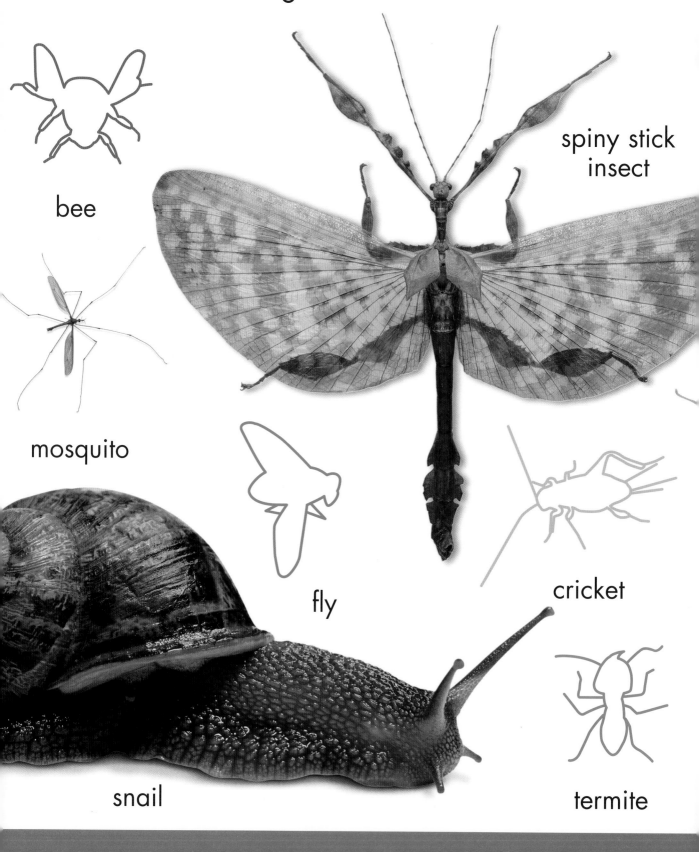

bee

spiny stick insect

mosquito

fly

cricket

snail

termite

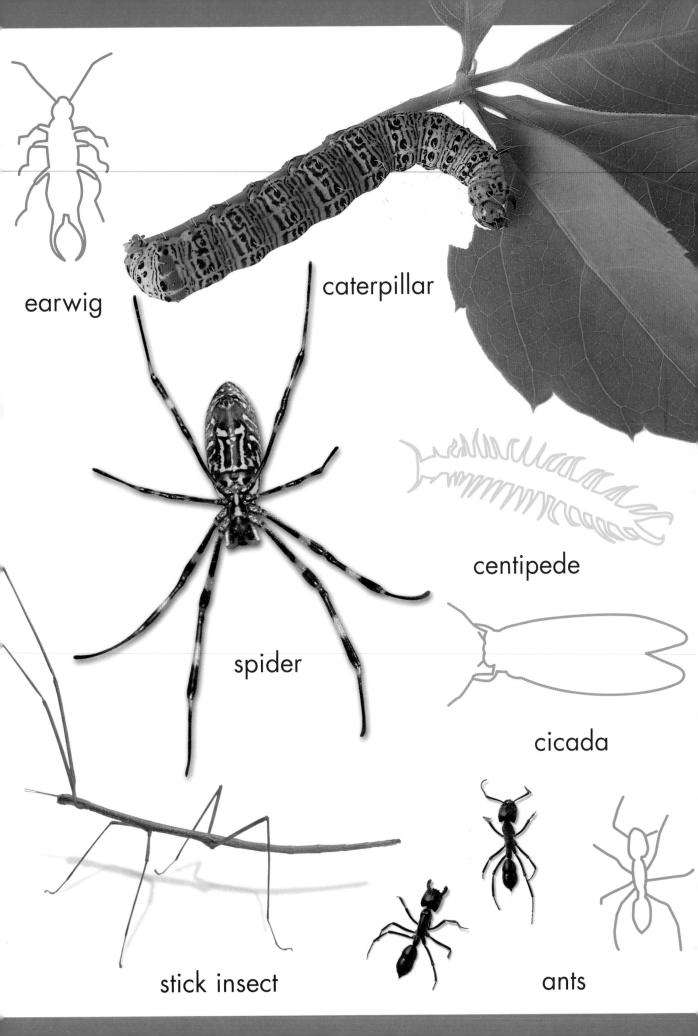

earwig

caterpillar

spider

centipede

cicada

stick insect

ants

Look closer!

Take a closer look at these insects and bugs.
Can you see which goes with which?

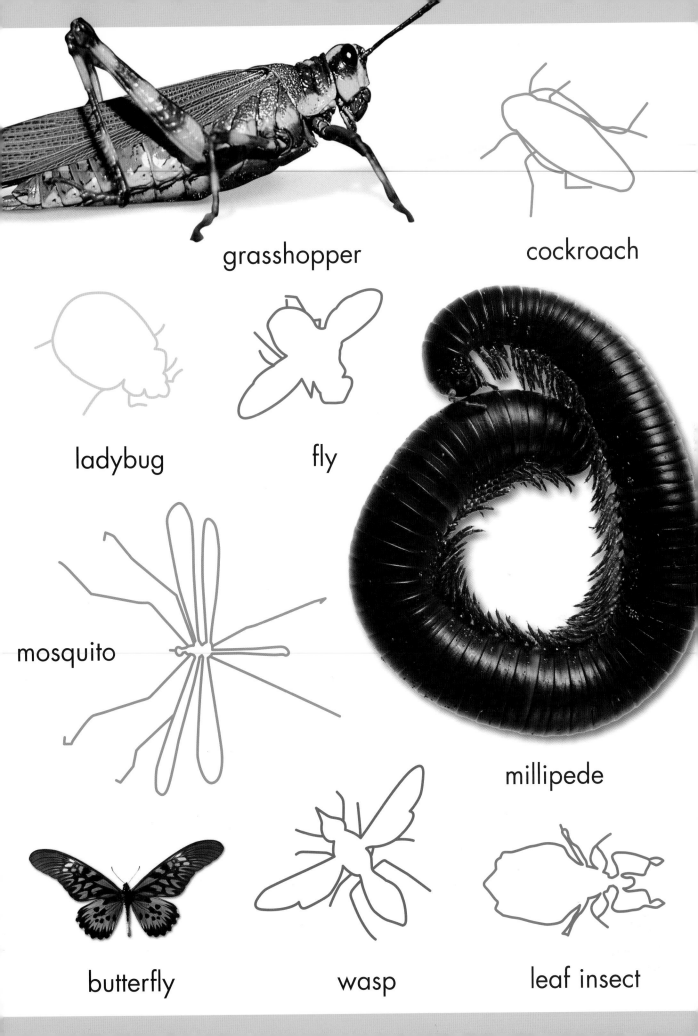

grasshopper

cockroach

ladybug

fly

mosquito

millipede

butterfly

wasp

leaf insect

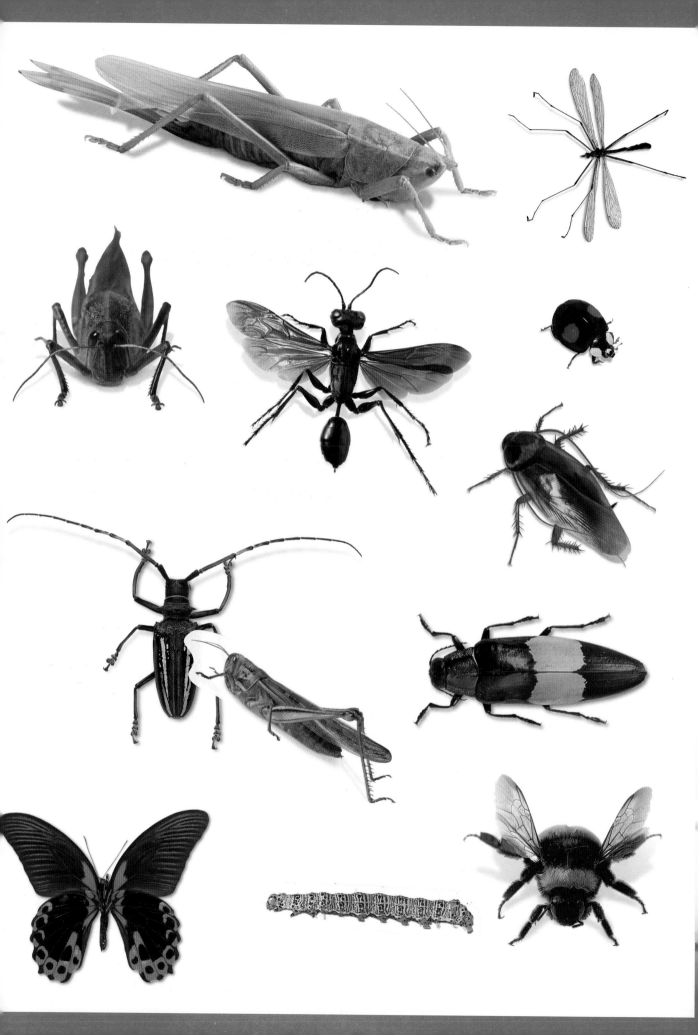

Zoom

Use the stickers at the end of this section to complete each page.

Sports cars

These cars can go very fast. Can you find the missing sports cars?

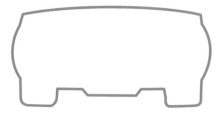

Jet fighters

Jet fighters are sleek and speedy.
They can travel faster than sound!

Motorcycles

Motorcycles are vehicles with two wheels.
Motorcycle riders must wear a helmet!

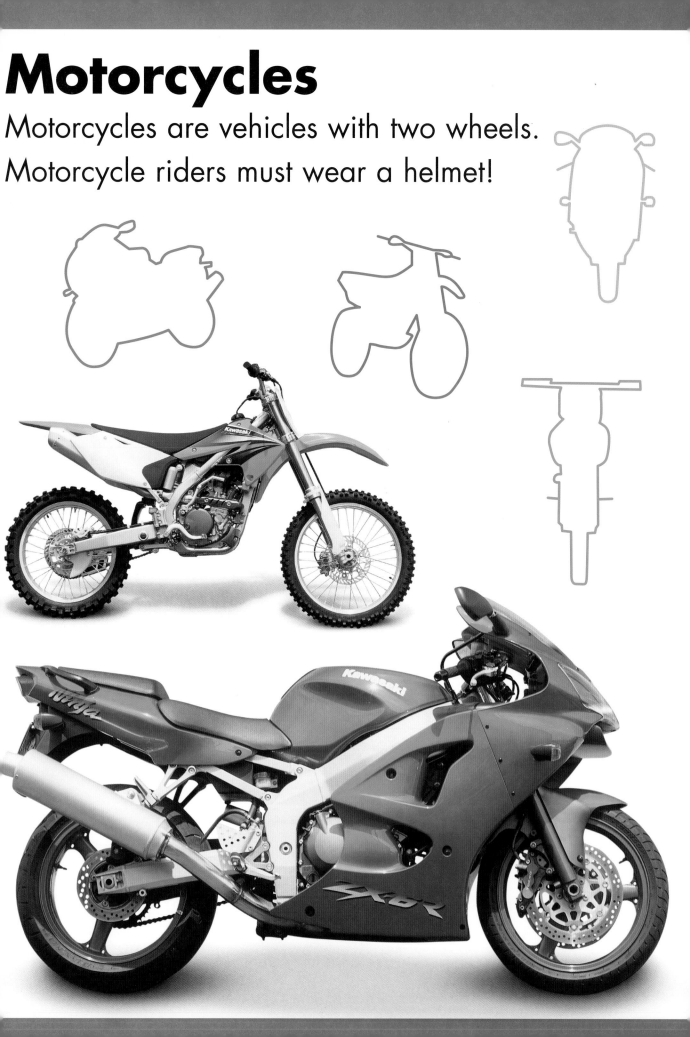

Quads

A quad bike is a four-wheeled all-terrain vehicle.
It is more stable at slow speeds.

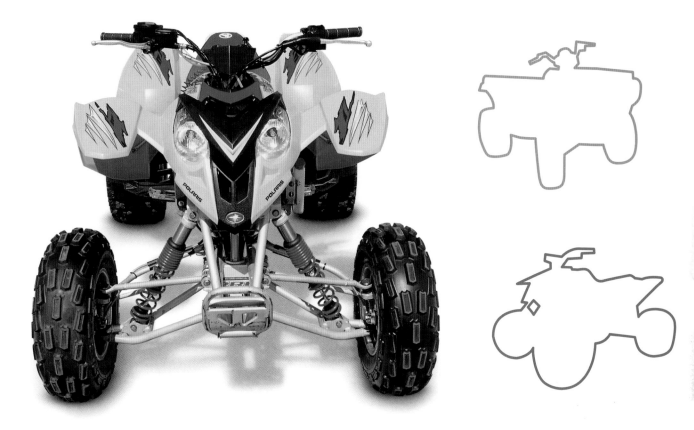

Hot rods

Which hot rod do you
think looks the coolest?

Trains

There are many different types of trains. They all zoom along tracks delivering passengers and goods.

Passenger planes

These aircraft are huge and powerful.
They fly many people great distances.

Racing cars

Racing cars zoom around a racing track trying to be first across the finish line. Can you find the missing racing cars?

Reptiles

Use the stickers at the end of this section to complete each page.

Lizards

Lizards are great climbers. Some lizards can grow up to 10 feet long!

This lizard looks like a prickly plant!

Alligators and crocodiles

These huge reptiles are great swimmers.
They have powerful jaws
and sharp teeth.

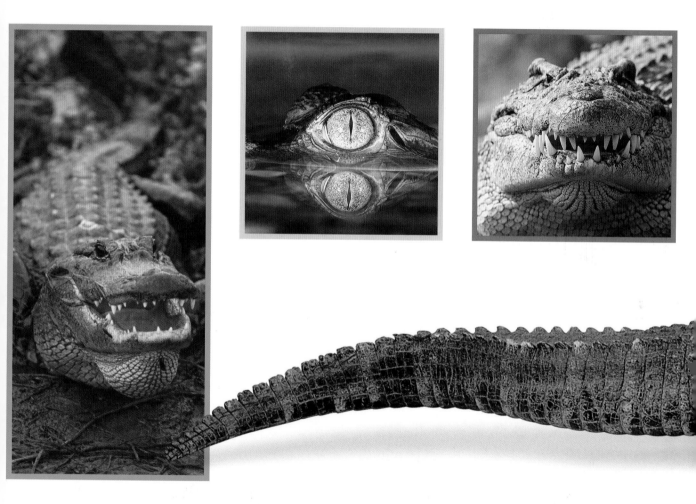

Snakes

Snakes are legless reptiles. Some snakes have a poisonous bite while others suffocate their prey.

Snakes use their tongues to smell.

Can you see the snake
in this picture?

Amphibians

These frogs and toads love water and are closely related to reptiles. Paste the matching sticker over the black and white photo.

Tortoises and turtles

Tortoises and turtles have a special shell that shields their body from danger.

Python

The python is a very powerful snake
that constricts its prey. Some species of
python can grow over 30 feet long!

Animal disguises

Many animals disguise themselves so predators cannot find them. Other animals, such as snakes, disguise themselves to sneak up on potential food! Can you see the hidden creatures?

The chameleon

The chameleon is an amazing lizard. It can change the color of its skin so that it blends in with its surroundings. Find the missing stickers to reveal this amazing lizard.

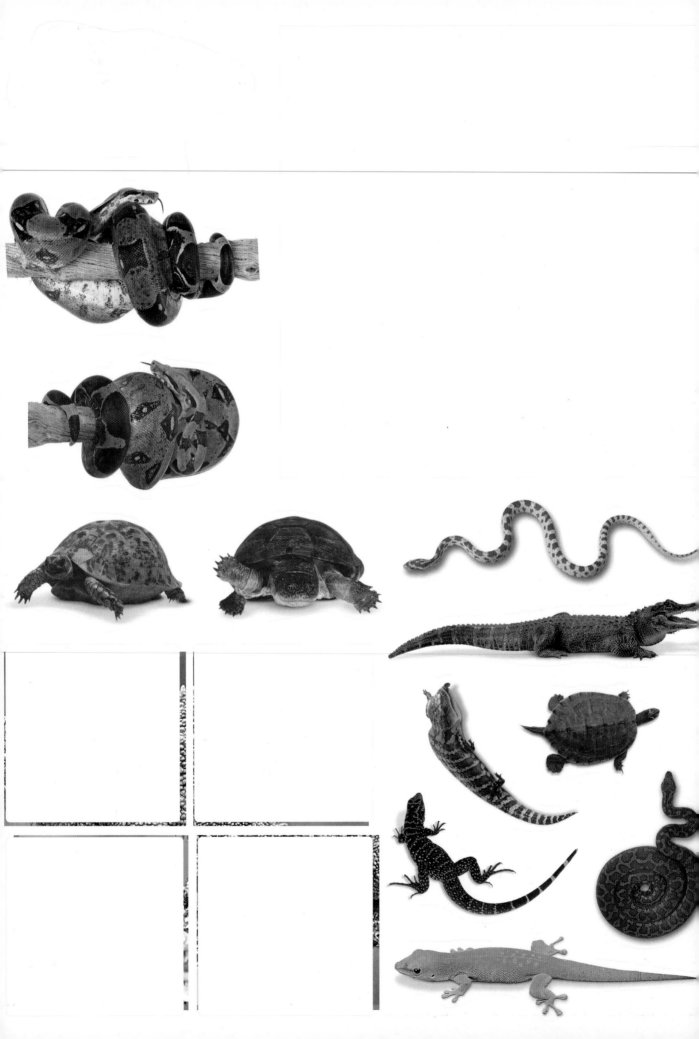

Emergency

Use the stickers at the end of this section to complete each page.

Fire engine

A fire engine is the vehicle that carries fire fighters and their equipment to an emergency.

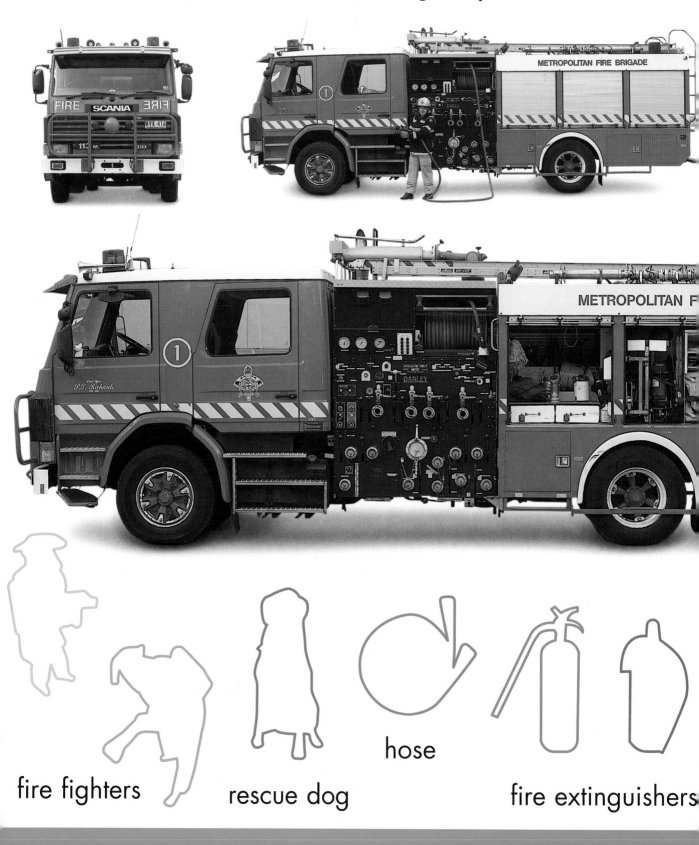

fire fighters

rescue dog

hose

fire extinguishers

Fire fighters can climb the ladder to rescue trapped people.

Air ambulance

This emergency aircraft can reach people that are far from the city. Can you find the missing air ambulances?

Ambulance

An ambulance takes sick or hurt people to hospital. Ambulances carry special equipment that can save lives.

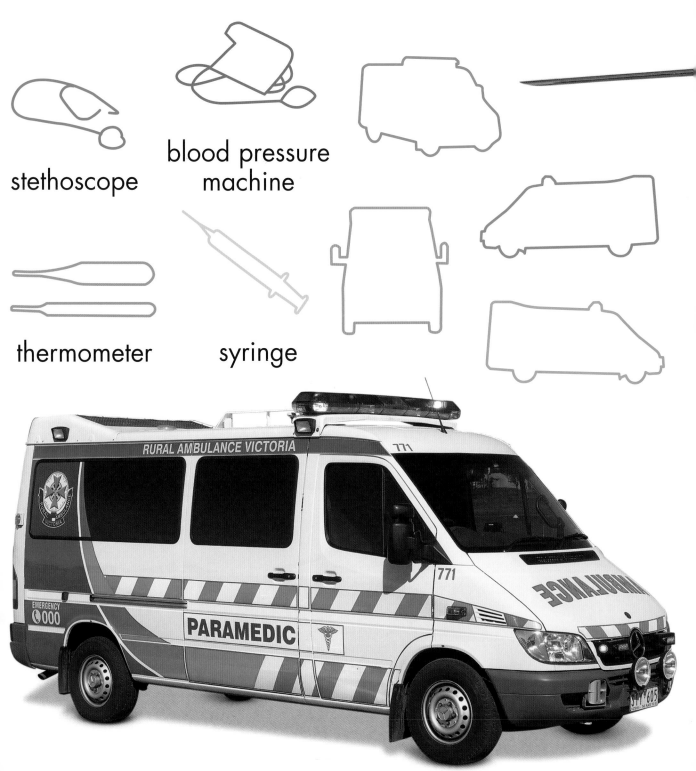

stethoscope

blood pressure machine

thermometer

syringe

RURAL AMBULANCE VICTORIA

771

771

EMERGENCY
📞 000

PARAMEDIC

AMBULANCE

Fire fighting helicopter

A fire fighting helicopter is able to put out fires from the air.

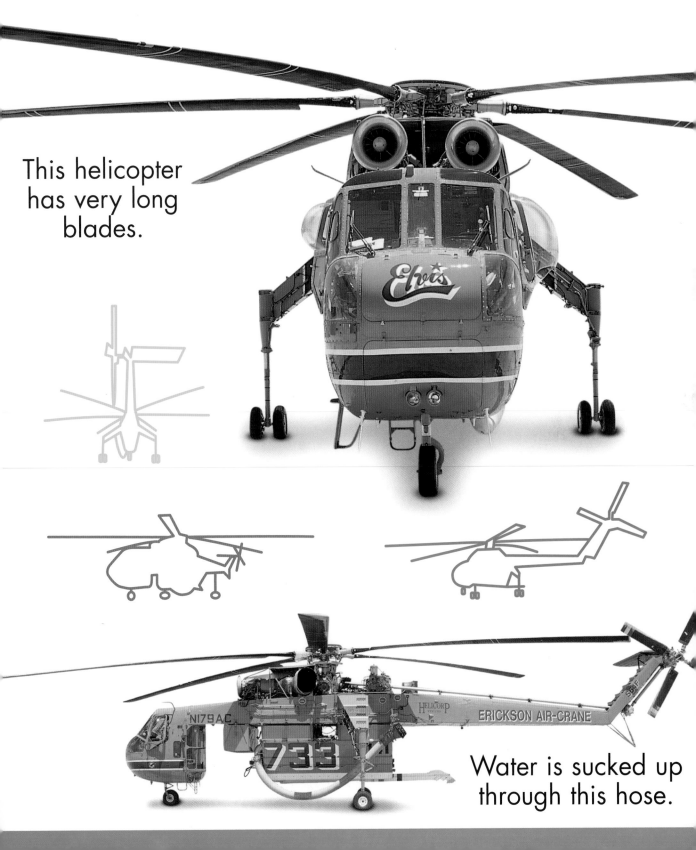

This helicopter has very long blades.

Water is sucked up through this hose.

Snowplow

The snowplow is a large vehicle used in snowy conditions. It is used to clear huge amounts of snow that block streets or railroads.

Rescue boat

A rescue boat is used to carry supplies, rescue injured people or locate ships. Most rescue boats travel at very fast speeds.

Police helicopter

A police helicopter is sometimes used as a police air patrol. Can you find the stickers that are missing from this page?

Fire fighter transport bus

These vehicles are used to transport fire fighters.
Can you find the missing fire fighting equipment?

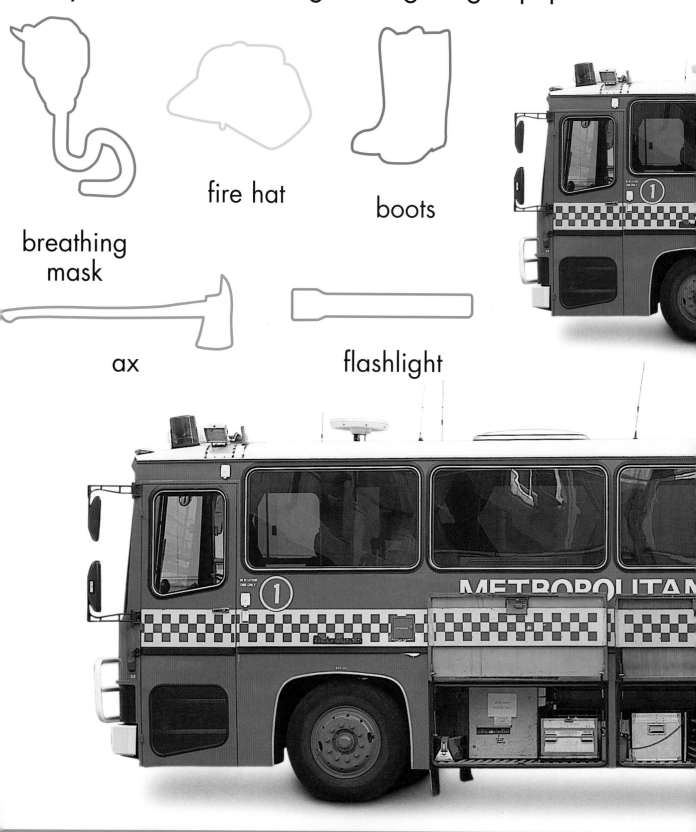

breathing mask

fire hat

boots

ax

flashlight

Police car

The police car is a vehicle used by the police. Police cars are equipped with radio-telephony – a system for communicating.

hat

handcuffs

whistle

badge

Airport fire engine

The airport fire engine travels very fast in an emergency.

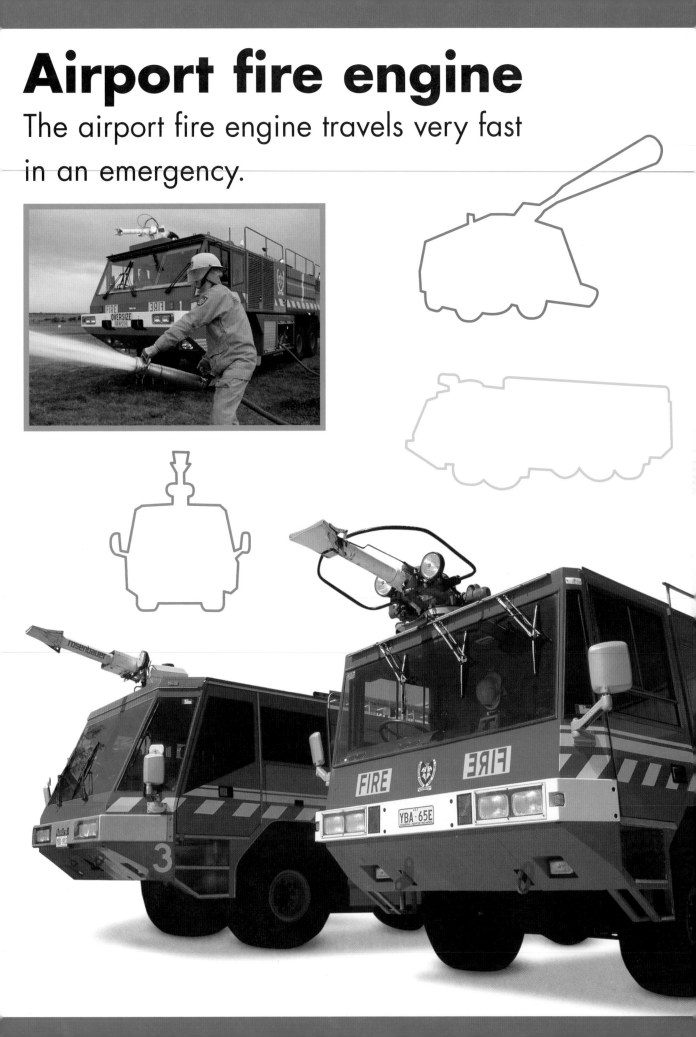

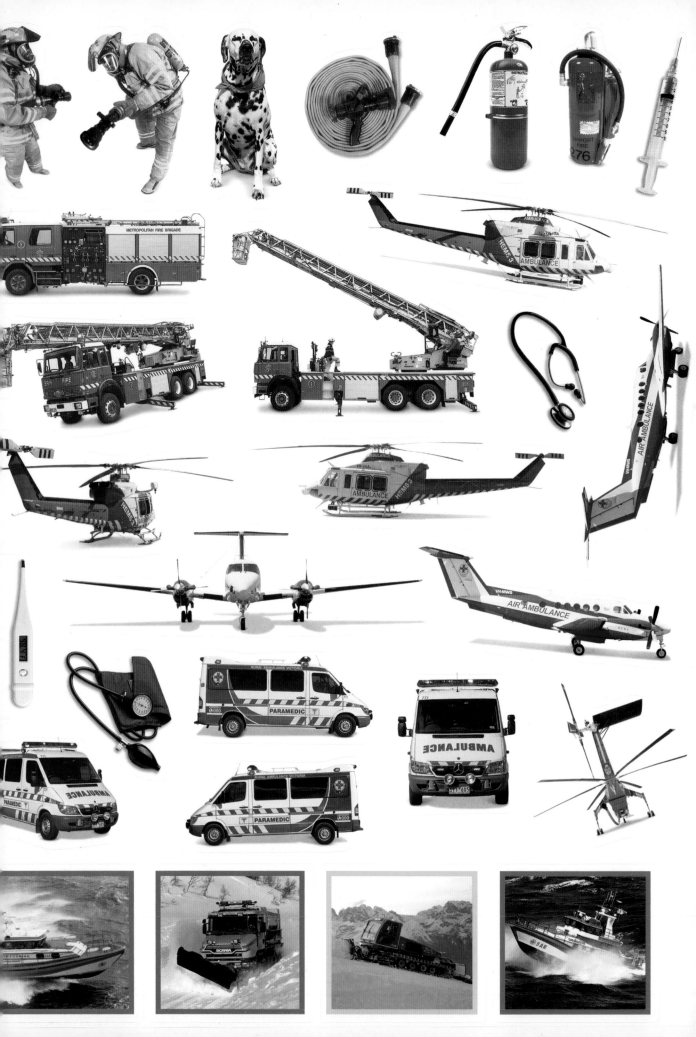

Sea Creatures

Use the stickers at the end of this section to complete each page.

Fish

There are thousands of species of fish in the ocean.
They come in many shapes and colors.

Sharks

Sharks are a type of large fish. Most sharks are not dangerous to humans.

The whale shark above is huge, and harmless! It grows over 50 feet long.

The giant basking shark is in danger of being extinct!

Seahorses

Seahorses are a type of fish that can be found all over the world. Seahorses are endangered due to overfishing.

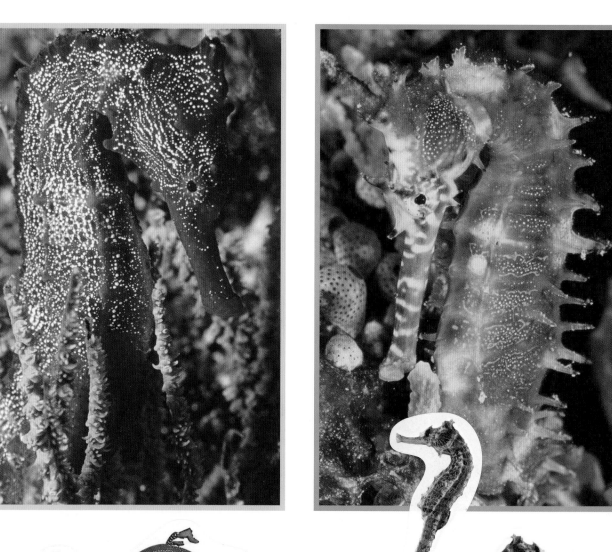

The sea dragon is a member of the seahorse family.

Back to school!

A group of fish swimming together is called a school. Can you find the missing fish?

Under the sea

Look at all the coral and fish! Can you find the diver taking photographs?